NIGHT-CROSSING

DEREK MAHON

Night-Crossing

LONDON
OXFORD UNIVERSITY PRESS
NEW YORK TORONTO
1968

Oxford University Press, Ely House, London W.1

GLASGOW NEW YORK TORONTO MELBOURNE WELLINGTON
CAPE TOWN SALISBURY IBADAN NAIROBI LUSAKA ADDIS ABABA
BOMBAY CALCUTTA MADRAS KARACHI LAHORE DACCA
KUALA LUMPUR HONG KONG TOKYO

© *Oxford University Press* 1968

PRINTED IN GREAT BRITAIN BY
THE BOWERING PRESS, PLYMOUTH

For Michael and Edna Longley

Acknowledgements

Acknowledgements are due to the Editors of the following periodicals in which some of these poems first appeared: *The Cheltenham Festival of Literature Programme, The Dublin Magazine, Icarus, The Irish Times, Northern Review, Outposts, Phoenix, Poetry Ireland,* and *The Poetry Review*; and to the B.B.C. (Northern Ireland). Some of the poems have also appeared in pamphlets published by Festival Publications of Belfast and the Erato Press, Cambridge, Massachusetts.

Contents

Girls in their Seasons

GIRLS in their seasons. Solstice and equinox,
This year, make reincarnate
Spry ghosts I had consigned to fate,
Left soaking at the ends of bars,
Pasted in dying calendars
Or locked in clocks.

I can no longer walk the streets at night
But under a lamp-post by a bistro,
To the sound of a zither,
I see one standing in an arc of snow,
Her collar up against the wintry weather
Smoking a cigarette.

Or, as now, slumped by a train window,
The hair of another flies in the air-stream.
This one is here in an advisory
Capacity, reminding me
Of a trip I took last winter
From dream into bad dream.

Their ghosts go with me as I hurtle north
Into the night,
Gathering momentum, age,
Know-how, experience (I travel light)—
Girls, you are welcome to my luggage
For what it is worth.

No earthly schedule can predict
Accurately our several destinations.
All we can do is wash and dress
And keep ourselves intact.
Besides which, this is an express
And passes all the stations.

Now we are running out of light and love,
Having left far behind
By-pass and fly-over.
The moon is no longer there
And matches go out in the wind.
Now all we have

Is the flinty chink of Orion and the Plough
And the incubators of a nearby farm
To light us through to the land of never-never.
Girls all, be with me now
And keep me warm
Before we go plunging into the dark for ever.

In Carrowdore Churchyard

at the grave of Louis MacNeice

YOUR ashes will not stir, even on this high ground,
However the wind tugs, the headstones shake—
This plot is consecrated, for your sake,
To what lies in the future tense. You lie
Past tension now, and spring is coming round
Igniting flowers on the peninsula.

Your ashes will not fly, however the rough winds burst
Through the wild brambles and the reverend trees.
All we may ask of you we have. The rest
Is not for publication, will not be heard.
Maguire, I believe, suggested a blackbird
And over your grave a phrase from Euripides.

Which suits you down to the ground, like this churchyard
With its play of shadow, its humane perspective.
Locked in the winter's fist, these hills are hard
As nails, yet soft and feminine in their turn
When fingers open and the hedges burn.
This, you implied, is how we ought to live—

The ironical, loving crush of roses against snow,
Each fragile, solving ambiguity. So
From the pneumonia of the ditch, from the ague
Of the blind poet and the bombed-out town you bring
The all-clear to the empty holes of spring,
Rinsing the choked mud, keeping the colours new.

SLOWLY, with the important carelessness
Of your kind, each spirit-sculptured face
Appears before me—eyes
Bleak from discoveries.

I had almost forgotten you had been,
So jealous was I of my skin
And the world with me. How
Goes it with you now?

Did death and its transitions disappoint you,
And the worms you so looked forward to?
Perhaps you found that you had to *queue*
For a ticket into hell,
Despite your sprays of laurel.

You were all children in your helpless wisdom,
Retiring loud-mouths who would not be dumb—
Frustrated rural clergymen
Nobody would ordain.

Then ask no favour of reincarnation,
No yearning after the booze and whores—
For you, if anyone,
Have played your part
In holding nature up to art . . .

Be content to sprawl in your upland meadows,
Hair and boy-mouths stuck with flowers—
And rest assured, the day
Will be all sunlight, and the night
A dutiful spectrum of stars.

Glengormley

for Padraic Fiacc

WONDERS are many and none is more wonderful than man
Who has tamed the terrier, trimmed the hedge
And grasped the principle of the watering can.
Clothes-pegs litter the window-ledge
And the long ships lie in clover. Washing lines
Shake out white linen over the chalk thanes.

Now we are safe from monsters, and the giants
Who tore up sods twelve miles by six
And hurled them out to sea to become islands
Can worry us no more. The sticks
And stones that once broke bones will not now harm
A generation of such sense and charm.

Only words hurt us now. No saint or hero,
Landing at night from the conspiring seas,
Brings dangerous tokens to the new era—
Their sad names linger in the histories.
The unreconciled, in their metaphysical pain,
Strangle on lamp-posts in the dawn rain

And much dies with them. I should rather praise
A worldly time under this worldly sky—
The terrier-taming, garden-watering days
Those heroes pictured as they struggled through
The quick noose of their finite being. By
Necessity, if not choice, I live here too.

In Belfast

WALKING among my own this windy morning
In a tide of sunlight between shower and shower,
I resume my old conspiracy with the wet
Stone and the unwieldy images of the squinting heart.
Once more, as before, I remember not to forget.

There is a perverse pride in being on the side
Of the fallen angels and refusing to get up.
We could *all* be saved by keeping an eye on the hill
At the top of every street, for there it is—
Eternally, if irrelevantly, visible—

But yield instead to the humorous formulae,
The spurious mystery in the knowing nod.
Or we keep sullen silence in light and shade,
Rehearsing our astute salvations under
The cold gaze of a sanctimonious God.

One part of my mind must learn to know its place—
The things that happen in the kitchen-houses
And echoing back-streets of this desperate city
Should engage more than my casual interest,
Exact more interest than my casual pity.

Grandfather

THEY brought him in on a stretcher from the world,
Wounded but humorous. And he soon recovered—
Boiler-rooms, row upon row of gantries rolled
Away to reveal the landscape of a childhood
Only he can recapture. Even on cold
Mornings he is up at six with a block of wood
Or a box of nails, descreetly up to no good
Or banging round the house like a four-year-old—
Never there when you call. But after dark
You hear his great boots thumping in the hall
And in he comes, as cute as they come. Each night
His shrewd eyes bolt the door and set the clock
Against the future, then his light goes out—
Nothing escapes him. He escapes us all.

My Wicked Uncle

It was my first funeral.
Some loss of status as a nephew since
Dictates that I recall
My numbness, my grandfather's hesitance,
My five aunts busy in the hall.

I found him closeted with living souls—
Coffined to perfection in the bedroom.
Death had deprived him of his mustache,
His thick horn-rimmed spectacles,
The easy corners of his salesman dash
(Those things by which I had remembered him)
And sundered him behind unnatural gauze.
His hair was badly parted on the right
As if for Sunday school. That night
I saw my uncle as he really was.

The narrative he dispensed was mostly
Wicked avuncular fantasy—
He went in for waistcoats and haircream.
But something about him
Demanded that you picture the surprise
Of the chairman of the board, when to
'What will you have with your whiskey?' my uncle replies—
'Another whiskey, please.'

Once he was jailed in New York
Twice on the same day—
The crookedest chief steward in the Head Line.
And once (he affected communism)
He brought the whole crew out on strike
In protest at the loss of a day's pay
Crossing the international date line.

They buried him slowly above the sea,
The young Presbyterian minister,
Rumpled and windy in the sea air.
A most absorbing ceremony—
Ashes to ashes, dust to dust.
I saw sheep huddled in the long wet grass
Of the golf-course, and the empty freighters
Sailing for ever down Belfast Lough
In a fine rain, their sirens going,
As the gradual graph of my uncle's life and
Times dipped precipitately
Into the bowels of Carnmoney Cemetery.

His teenage kids are growing horns and claws—
More wicked already than ever my uncle was.

Death of a Film-Star

If it were said, let there be no more light,
Let rule the wide winds and the long-tailed seas,
Then she would die in all our hearts tonight—
Till when, her image broods over the cities
In negative, for in the darkness she is bright,
Caught in a pose of infinite striptease.

Goddesses, from the whipped sea or the slums,
Will understand her final desolate
Stark-nakedness, her teeth ground to the gums,
Fingernails filthy, siren hair in spate
(And always with her, as she goes and comes,
Her little bottle of barbiturate)—

For she was one of them, queen among the trash,
Cinders swept to the palace from her shack
By some fairy godmother. In a flash
Spirited to the front row from the back.
Stars last so long before they go scattering ash
Down the cold back-streets of the zodiac—

Fall and dissolve into the thickening air,
Burning the black ground of the negative.
We are slowly learning from meteors like her
Who have learnt how to shrivel and let live,
That when an immovable body meets an ir-
Resistible force, something has got to give.

Spring Letter in Winter

Two years on and none the wiser
I go down to the door in the morning twilight.
I have been half awake all night
Hearing the grey snow gather on the horizon,
The danse macabre of leaf-skeletons.

And there it is—alone, a swallow
Back from the warm south, pleading
Silently to be opened. My hands are
Tearing the white folds, perhaps there is
Still time, perhaps there is still time . . .

Postman, postman, you have done well
To bring me this reprieve. Those frozen
Runways, windy skies could not suspect
The bright reception at the end of all.
This darkness is the darkness of nightfall—

But now, suddenly, snowdrop and crocus
Are flowering quickly under the shining birches.
This odd incursion is familiar.
Water is flowing where no river was or
I have come early to the sea in spring.

Body and Soul

BODY is soul, soul body—
Your body is lake water.

Light breaks where it goes in,
Breaks to a water rhythm.

Body is open house, and no
Ghosts that are not woven

Into the very carpets,
The wallpaper, the woodwork.

There are no trapped starlings
Beating against the windows,

Running behind the armchairs,
Crashing into the clock.

Only a swallow out of Bede
Dives through the dining-room—

The shadow of a straight line
Reflected in your eyes.

Preface to a Love Poem

THIS is a circling of itself and you—
A form of words, compact and compromise,
   Prepared in the false dawn of the half-true
Beyond which the shapes of truth materialize.
   This is a blind with sunlight filtering through.

This is a stirring in the silent hours,
As lovers do with thoughts they cannot frame
   Or leave, but bring to darkness like night-flowers,
Words never choosing but the words choose them—
   Birds crowing, wind whistling off pale stars.

This is a night-cry, neither here nor there—
A spooky echo from the clamorous dead
   Who cried aloud in anger and despair
Outlasting stone and bronze, but took instead
   Their wan smiles underground with them for ever.

This is at one remove—a substitute
For final answers. But the wise man knows
   To cleave to the one living absolute
Beyond paraphrase, and shun a shrewd repose.
   The words are aching in their own pursuit

To say *I love you* out of indolence,
As one might speak at sea without forethought,
   Drifting inconsequently among islands.
This is a way of airing my distraught
   Love of your silence. You are the soul of silence.

Bird Sanctuary

for Jill Schlesinger

TOWARDS sleep I came
Upon the place again,
Its paper sea and tame
Eddying wind. The mist and rain
Come only after dark, and then
Steam out to sea at dawn.

I have erected
A bird sanctuary, to hold
The loaded world in check.
This is where all my birds collect—
Cormorant, puffin and kittiwake
All duly enrolled.

I live elsewhere—
In a city down the coast
Composed of earth and fire.
At night I walk beside the river
So that the elements of air
And water are not lost.

I expect great things
Of these angels of wind,
Females, males, and fledgelings.
The sudden whirring of their wings
Disturbs the noon, and midnight rings
With echoes from their island.

Will come a time
When they sit on the housetops

Shouting, thousands of them,
This is their own, their favourite dream
Beyond reason, beyond rhyme
So that the heart stops.

De Quincey in Later Life

TONIGHT the blessed state, that long repose
Where time is measured
Not by the clock but by the hours
Of the wind. His seventh heaven when it snows
The valley under, and the frosty stars
Sing to his literary leisure.

Hearth rugs, a tea-pot and a quart
Decanter of laudanum—
Perihelion of paradise. No sort
Or condition of men but is the less human
For want of this. *Mens sana
In corpore sano.*

Excellent as an antidote for toothache
And the busy streets. Wood crackles better
In a head removed, and fresh water
Springs wiselier in a heart that is not sick . . .
And then the dreams came, and his children
Woke him every day at noon—

Until he cried out I WILL SLEEP NO MORE
And quit the hot sheets and the enormous
Apparitions dying on the floor.
He left the house,
Walked out to the sunlight on the hill
And heard, in the whispering-gallery of his soul,

His own small, urgent discord echoing back
From the dark roads of abandon
And the restless thunder of London—
Where he had gone in his eighteenth year
And walked the terraces after dark,
Seeking precisely some such panacea.

Four Walks in the Country near Saint Brieuc

I. *Early Morning*

No doubt the creation was like this—
Slower than time, spectacular only in size,
Revealing coldly what there is of chaos.
First there is darkness, then somehow light.
We call this day and the other night
And watch in vain for the second of sunrise.

Suddenly, near at hand, the click of a wooden shoe—
An old woman among the primeval shapes
Abroad in the field of light, sombrely dressed.
She calls good-day, since there are bad days too,
And her eyes go down. She has seen perhaps
Ten thousand dawns like this, and is not impressed.

II. *Man and Bird*

ALL fly away at my approach
As they have done time out of mind,
And hide in the thicker leaves to watch
The shadowy ingress of mankind.

My whistle-talk does not disarm
Presuppositions of ill-will—
Although they rarely come to harm
The ancient fear is in them still.

Which irritates my *amour-propre*
As an enlightened alien,
And renders yet more wide the gap
From their world to the world of men.

17

So perhaps they have something after all—
Either we shoot them out of hand
Or parody them with a bird-call
Neither of us can understand.

III. *After Midnight*

THEY are all round me in the dark
With claw-knives for my sleepy anarch—

Beasts of the fields, birds of the air,
Their slit-eyes glittering everywhere.

I am man self-made, self-made man,
No small-talk now for those who ran

In and out of my dirty childhood.
We have grown up as best we could.

They would gnaw my body to the bone
But know, as I know, I am not alone.

IV. *Exit Molloy*

Now at the end I smell the smells of spring
Where in a dark ditch I lie wintering—
And the little town only a mile away,
Happy and fatuous in the light of day.
A bell tolls gently. I should start to cry
But my eyes are closed and my face dry.
I am not important and I have to die.
Strictly speaking, I am already dead,
But still I can hear the birds sing on over my head.

Van Gogh among the Miners

for Colin Middleton

SHIVERING in the darkness
Of pits, slag-heaps, beetroot fields,
I gasp for light and life
Like a caged bird in spring-time
Banging the bright bars.

Like a glow-worm I move among
The caged Belgian miners,
And the light on my forehead
Is the dying light of truth.
God gutters down to metaphor—

A subterranean tapping, light
Refracted in a glass of beer
As if through a church window,
Or a basin ringed with coal-dust
After the ritual evening bath.

Theo, I am discharged for being
Over-zealous, they call it,
And not dressing the part.
In time I shall go south
And paint what I have seen—

A meteor of golden light
On chairs, faces and old boots,
Setting fierce fire to the eyes
Of sun-flowers and fishing boats,
Each one a miner in disguise.

The Forger

WHEN I sold my fake Vermeers to Goering
Nobody knew, nobody guessed
The agony, the fanaticism
Of working beyond criticism
And better than the best.

When they hauled me before the war-crimes tribunal
No one suspected, nobody knew
The agony of regrets
With which I told my secrets.
They missed the point, of course—
To hell with the national heritage,
I sold my *soul* for potage.

The experts were good value, though,
When they went to work on my studio—
Not I, but *they* were the frauds.
I revolutionized their methods.

Now, nothing but claptrap
About mere technique and true vision,
As if there were a distinction—
Their way of playing it down.
But my genius will live on,
For even at one remove
The thing I meant was love—

And I, too, have wandered
In the dark streets of Holland,
With hunger at my belly
When the mists rolled in from the sea.

And I, too, have suffered
Obscurity and derision,
And sheltered in my heart of hearts
A light to transform the world.

Day Trip to Donegal

for Paul Smyth

WE reached the sea in early afternoon,
Climbed stiffly out. There were urgent things to be done—
Clothes to be picked up, people to be seen.
As ever, the nearby hills were a deeper green
Than anywhere in the world, and the grave
Grey of the sea the grimmer in that enclave.

Down at the pier the boats gave up their catch—
Torn mouths and spewed-up lungs. They fetch
Ten times as much in the city as there,
And still the fish come in year after year—
Herring and whiting, flopping about the deck
In attitudes of agony and heartbreak.

How could we hope to make them understand?
Theirs is a sea-mind, mindless upon land
And dead. Their systematic genocide
(Nothing remarkable that millions died)
To us is a necessity
For ours are land-minds, mindless in the sea.

We left at eight, drove back the way we came,
The sea receding down each muddy lane.
Around midnight we changed-down into suburbs
Sunk in a sleep no gale-force wind disturbs.
The time of year had left its mark
On frosty pavements glistening in the dark.

Give me a ring, goodnight, and so to bed ...
That night the slow sea washed against my head,
Performing its immeasurable erosions—

Spilling into the skull, marbling the stones
That spine the very harbour wall,
Uttering its threat to villages of landfall.

At dawn I was alone far out at sea
Without skill or reassurance (nobody
To show me how, no earnest of rescue),
Cursing my mindless failure to take due
Forethought for this, contriving vain
Overtures to the mindless wind and rain.

Gipsies

for Nina Hutchinson

ONCE there was house and home
And books against the cold.
We are all gipsies now—
Pea-pickers, pickpockets,
Haters, procrastinators,
Wanderers in the salt dunes,
Tellers of strange fortunes,
Bathers in cold waters—
Sleeping, like John Clare,
With our feet to the pole star.

An Unborn Child

I HAVE already come to the verge of
Departure. A month or so and
I shall be vacating this familiar room.
Its fabric fits me almost like a glove
While leaving latitude for a free hand.
I begin to put on the manners of the world,
Sensing the splitting light above
My head, where in the silence I lie curled.

Certain mysteries are relayed to me
Through the dark network of my mother's body
While she sits sewing the white shrouds
Of my apotheosis. I know the twisted
Kitten that lies there sunning itself
Under the bare bulb, the clouds
Of goldfish mooning around upon the shelf—
In me these data are already vested.

I feel them in my bones—bones which embrace
Nothing, for I am completely egocentric.
The pandemonium of encumbrances
Which will absorb me, mind and senses—
Intricacies of the box and the rat-race—
I imagine only. Though they linger and,
Like fingers, stretch until the knuckles crack,
They cannot dwarf the dimensions of my hand.

I must compose myself in the nerve-centre
Of this metropolis, and not fidget—
Although sometimes at night, when the city
Has gone to sleep, I keep in touch with it
Listening to the warm red water

Racing in the sewers of my mother's body—
Or the moths, soft as eyelids, or the rain
Wiping its wet wings on the window-pane.

And sometimes too, in the small hours of the morning
When the dead filament has ceased to ring—
After the goldfish are dissolved in darkness
And the kitten has gathered itself up into a ball
Between the groceries and the sewing,
I slip the trappings of my harness
To range these hollows in discreet rehearsal
And, battering at the concavity of my caul,

Produce in my mouth the words I WANT TO LIVE—
This my first protest, and shall be my last.
As I am innocent, everything I do
Or say is couched in the affirmative.
I want to see, hear, touch and taste
These things with which I am to be encumbered.
Perhaps I need not worry—give
Or take a day or two, my days are numbered.

Canadian Pacific

FROM famine, pestilence and persecution
Those gaunt forefathers shipped abroad to find
Rough stone of heaven beyond the western ocean,
And staked their claim and pinned their faith.
Tonight their children whistle through the dark,
Frost chokes the windows. They will not have heard
The wild geese flying south over the lakes
While the lakes harden beyond grief and anger—
The eyes fanatical, rigid the soft necks,
The great wings sighing with a nameless hunger.

Recalling Aran

A dream of limestone in sea-light
Where gulls have placed their perfect prints.
Reflection in that final sky
Shames vision into simple sight—
Into pure sense, experience.
Four thousand miles away tonight,
Conceived beyond such innocence,
I clutch the memory still, and I
Have measured everything with it since.

Epitaph for Robert Flaherty

THE relief to be out of the sun—
To have travelled north once more
To my islands of dark ore,
Where winter is so long
Only a little light
Gets through, and that perfect.

April on Toronto Island

ONCE more to the island after the spring thaw—
A qualified silence, old snow under the
Boardwalks, for the winter dies hard.

The winter dies hard, and a last wintry reluctance
Clutches the splintered birches. There is
Nothing among the boarded-up houses,

Nothing along the lakeshore but bird-bones and fish-bones
Greasy with diesel oil, and the clapboard
Church of Saint Andrew-by-the-Lake.

There is not even a bird, although there are bird noises
And the growl of commerce, muted by empty
Distance, where the downtown skyline

Stands out like the first draft of a new civilization.
But the slick water mourns for its vanished
Ice like a lost child for its mother.

Another ferry pulls away from the landing-stage,
The lighthouse blows its now redundant
Fog-warning over the rocks and

Slowly, in ones and twos, the people are coming back
To stand on the thin beach among the
Washed-up flotsam of the winter,

Watching the long grainers move down to the seaway.
Their faces dream of other islands,
Clear cliffs and salt water,

Fields brighter than paradise in the first week of creation—
Grace caught in a wind or a tide, our
Lives in infinite preparation.

As God is my Judge

THEY said I got away in a boat
And humbled me at the inquiry. I tell you
    I sank as far that night as any
Hero. As I sat shivering on the dark water
    I turned to ice to hear my costly
Life go thundering down in a pandemonium of
    Prams, pianos, sideboards, winches,
Boilers bursting and shredded ragtime. Now I hide
    In a lonely house behind the sea
Where the tide leaves broken toys and hatboxes
    Silently at my door. The showers of
April, flowers of May mean nothing to me, nor the
    Late light of June, when my gardener
Describes to strangers how the old man keeps his bed
    On seaward mornings after nights of
Wind, and will see no one, repeat no one. Then it is
    I drown again with all those dim
Lost faces I never understood. My poor soul
    Screams out in the starlight, heart
Breaks loose and rolls down like a stone. Include me
    Honoris causa in your lamentations.

BRUCE ISMAY

31

The Prisoner

FOR several days I have been under
House-arrest. My table has become
A sundial to its empty bottle.
With wise abandon
Lover and friend have gone.

In the window opposite
An old lady sits each afternoon
Talking to no one. I shout.
Either she is deaf or
She has reason.

I have books, provisions, running water
And a little stove. It would not matter
If cars moved silently at night
And no light or laughter
Came from the houses down the street.

It is taking longer than almost anything—
But I know, when it is over
And back come friend and lover,
I shall forget it like a childhood illness
Or a sleepless night-crossing.

First Principles

THE one poem I want
To write will never feature
Women you meet in daydreams,
Perfect beyond nature,
Vermouth in sculptured hand,
Records and magazines—

Or praise poetic wives
Who leave hairs in the bath
And fart in bed, and remain
Loveable unto death.
They live their private lives
In the sun and the rain.

Nor will I settle
For innocence per se,
Blown hair and barren rock,
Heather and ocean spray—
With pew and pedestal
I will have no truck.

My poem will not send
Them into a quiet room
To thumb my books and kill
A rainy afternoon,
Or call a silly girl-friend
And yack about my soul—

No, it will so derange
The poor bitches, that they
Will come round on their knees
At all hours of the day,
Crippled with visceral rage
And croaking please, please.

The Poets Lie where they Fell

No REST for the wicked—
Curled up in armchairs
Or flat out on the floors
Of well-furnished apartments
Belonging to friends of friends,
We lie where we fell.

One more shiftless habit,
It joins the buttered books,
Stale loaves and wandering dishes,
The shirts in the oven
And the volcanic ashtray.
Forgive us. This is our way,

We were born to this—
Deckchairs, train corridors,
American bus stations,
Park benches, open boats
And wind-worried terraces
Of nineteenth-century Paris.

Forgive us. We mean well
To your wives' well-wrought ankles
Their anthropomorphic shoes.
We love your dying embers,
Your happy moonstruck bottles,
And we lie where we fell.

Back home in mid-morning
We wash, we change and drink
Coffee. Perhaps we sing.
Then off we go once more,
Smiling our secret smile and only
Slightly the worse for wear.

Legacies

after Villon

I

In the year fourteen fifty-six
Right at the very dead of winter,
The wolves hungry and the nights dark,
I, Francois Villon, clerk,
Ceasing to kick against the pricks
And acting on an urge to break
The yoke of love around my neck,
Decide to pull myself together.

So I do what I think is best
Since she, with no thought of disguise,
Observes with mild disinterest
The frantic longing in my eyes—
Which makes my soul cry out to heaven
For vengeance from those gods above
Whose duty is to shield the fallen
Lover from the knives of love.

And if I chose to misconstrue
A casual word or lingering glance
That charged my body through and through
As having some significance,
I have surely learnt my lesson now—
My heart is torn out by the root.
Now I must turn elsewhere and put
Some other pasture to the plough.

Well, I can find no cure at all,
My best bet is to go away.

Goodbye, good luck to one and all—
Tomorrow I take the road to Angers.
Say I was sacrificed for love
And died with all my parts intact.
Soon I shall be enrolled above
Among the amorous elect.

And since I have no choice but to go
And cannot vouch for my return
(I am not above reproach, I know,
Not being cast in bronze or iron—
Life is unsure, and death, we learn,
Gives no redress in any event)
For all those whom it may concern
I make this will and testament.

II

Item, to her who, as I said,
So cruelly discarded me
That now I feel my senses dead
And pleasure mere vacuity—
My broken heart, empty and numb,
For her to dispose of as she chooses.
Although she treated me like scum
God grant her the mercy she refuses.

Item, to master Jean Cornu
And master Ithier Marchand,
To whom some recompense is due—
My sword, as sharp as it is long,
Which at this moment lies in pawn,
That they may rescue it from thence
Before its time is overdue
And split two ways on the expense.

And out of pity I bequeath
To children starving in the snow
Something to bring them some relief—
I list three of their names below.
God help them, not a shirt nor shoe
Among the lot of them, poor things.
I want to help them struggle through
At least into the coming spring.

To Colin Laurence, first of all,
Jean Marceau and Girard Gossuin
Who have nothing whatever they can call
Their own, and wear what rags they can—
A sizeable cut of all my goods
Or sixpence each against the cold.
God knows what fancy wines and foods
May warm their hearts when I am old.

Item, to those in hospitals
The cobwebs from my window-pane,
To sleepers under market stalls
A smack in the eye and an aching brain—
And may they shiver there, morose
In tattered coat and battered hat,
Unshaven, thin and snotty-nosed,
Stiff as a board and soaking wet.

And to the barber I bequeath
My accumulated locks of hair,
And these in full and outright gift—
My old shoes to the shoemaker,
My old clothes to the ragman when
I finally get through with them,
Eaten away by moths and lice—
At rather less than retail price.

III

Well, I had got so far tonight,
Alone in the silence of my room
And being in the mood to write,
When interrupted by the boom
Of the great clock in the Sorbonne
Which rings the angelus at nine,
And put aside this will of mine
To pray, as I have always done.

When my devotions after a while
Grew still, and the mind, to my relief,
Returned, I turned again to the will
But found my inkwell frozen stiff
And my last candle burnt away—
So, muffled up in coat and hat,
I closed my eyes to sleep till day
And let my testament go at that.

Done at the aforesaid time of year
By Villon, of such great repute
He wastes away with cold and hunger,
Thin as a rake and black as soot.
All his possessions, tent and hut,
To various friends are given away—
All but a little change, and that
Will scarcely last beyond today.